SCHWARTZ

HOME COOKING
❧ FROM ❧
AROUND THE WORLD

© Schwartz Spices,
Dormer Road, Thame,
Oxfordshire OX9 3SL

Recipes: Cathy Chambers & Clare Billings
for the Schwartz Home Economics Division.

Photography: John Ash

Designed & Produced by:
Storrar & Sánchez, South Newington, Oxon.

Illustrations by Javier Sánchez

For further information:
SCHWARTZ SPICES, DORMER ROAD,
THAME, OXON OX9 3SL

Front cover: Paella.

CONTENTS

To keep your
Schwartz herbs and
spices in their prime
condition, make
sure you store them:
- in well sealed jars
- somewhere cool and dry
- away from direct sunlight to prevent fading.

Stored in this way, herbs and ground spices will have a life of around
18 months to 2 years, while whole spices will keep for between 3 and 5 years.

If you have any queries on the use of herbs and spices in cooking, just
write to the Schwartz Information Service which has been set up especially to
help you. Our team of experienced Home Economists will be only too pleased to
answer your questions or send you further information. Just write to:
Schwartz Information Service, Dormer Road, Thame, Oxon OX9 3SL.

"Home Cooking from Around the World"

"What shall I cook tonight?"

Everyone who cooks for family and friends needs a little inspiration for everyday meals and sometimes for more special occasions.

In "Home Cooking from Around the World" Schwartz have used their special knowledge of herbs and spices to give well known dishes from across the continents a new and exciting slant. Some of the recipes are quick and easy for day to day cooking, while others are a little more adventurous for entertaining.

The dishes range from exotic Spiced Lamb and Aubergine Koftas to very British, but equally mouthwatering, Bread and Butter Pudding. "Home Cooking from Around the World" explores a vast range of flavours – from the hot and aromatic spices which grow near the Equator, to the cool and fragrant herbs of the Mediterranean.

With over 150 years of experience in sourcing and buying the best crops, Schwartz herbs and spices are always of the finest quality. After careful selection, they are thoroughly cleaned and purified. Our special milling processes for the spices help to retain the essential oils which give them their wonderful taste and smell. Careful packing into well sealed glass jars, moisture proof sachets and drums ensures a perfect product just ready for you to release the marvellous aromas and flavours into your cooking.

Recipe Notes

All recipes have been developed and tested using accurate spoon measures. All measures given are level.

Key to Symbols

15 mins

The chopping knife sign followed by a time indicates the approximate preparation time. Any additional time (e.g. marinating, chilling) is also indicated.

❋

The snowflake sign indicates whether the recipe is suitable for freezing. The absence of this sign indicates that the recipe is not suitable for freezing.

1 hour

The saucepan sign followed by a time, indicates the approximate cooking time.

Cals 410

Approximate calorie counts have been calculated per serving for each recipe.

Devilled Chicken left, Chicken Piri Piri right, see over for recipes.

Chicken
& Turkey

Chicken & Turkey

Serves 4

Devilled CHICKEN

For the marinade:

6 tbs (90ml) tomato ketchup
4 tbs (60ml) Worcestershire sauce
4 tsp (20ml) mustard powder
4 tsp (20ml) Schwartz Hot Paprika
2 tsp (10ml) Schwartz Turmeric
2 tsp (10ml) clear honey
½ tsp (2.5ml) salt

1lb (450g) chicken wings – tips removed,
    or 8 chicken drumsticks – scored
2 tsp (10ml) Schwartz Poppy Seeds,
    Sesame Seeds or Mustard Seeds

    Blend the marinade ingredients together, pour over the chicken and refrigerate for 30 minutes or overnight.

    Cook the chicken pieces under a preheated grill, allowing approximately 10 minutes for wings and 30 minutes for drumsticks. Turn occasionally and baste with any remaining marinade throughout cooking. Just before the end of cooking, sprinkle with the Poppy, Sesame or Mustard Seeds.

    Also suitable for barbecuing.

Cals 230 10 mins + 30 mins marinating 10–30 mins

Serves 4

CHICKEN Piri Piri

For the marinade:

¼ pint (150ml) olive oil
2 tbs (30ml) lemon juice
2 tsp (10ml) Schwartz Crushed Chillies
1 tsp (5ml) Schwartz Garlic Salt
½ tsp (2.5ml) Schwartz Citrus Pepper
½ tsp (2.5ml) Schwartz Tarragon
½ tsp (2.5ml) Schwartz Basil

¼ tsp (1.25ml) Schwartz Oregano
¼ tsp (1.25ml) Schwartz Ground Bay
    Leaves

8 chicken drumsticks – skinned

    Place the marinade ingredients in a bowl and mix together. Score the chicken using a sharp knife, pour over the marinade, cover and refrigerate for 2 hours or overnight.

    Cook the chicken pieces under a preheated grill for 25-30 minutes, turning occasionally and basting with any remaining marinade throughout cooking.

    Serve hot with a mixed salad or fresh vegetables.

    Also suitable for barbecuing.

Cals 447 10 mins + 2 hrs marinating 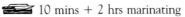 30 mins

FRANCE

Serves 4

CHICKEN *Chasseur*

2 tbs (30ml) cooking oil
4 chicken portions
6oz (175g) button onions – peeled
½ pint (300ml) dry white wine
½ pint (300ml) chicken stock
2 Schwartz Bay Leaves
¾ tsp (3.75ml) Schwartz Rosemary
¾ tsp (3.75ml) Schwartz Thyme
½ tsp (2.5ml) Schwartz Ground Black
   Pepper

¼ tsp (1.25ml) Schwartz Minced Garlic
½ tsp (2.5ml) salt
1 tbs (15ml) tomato purée
1 tsp (5ml) brown sugar
4oz (100g) button mushrooms
Cornflour paste – to thicken

Preheat oven to 350°F, 180°C, Gas Mark 4.
    Heat the oil in a frying pan and fry the chicken and onions until golden. Transfer to a casserole dish using a slotted spoon. Blend together the wine, stock, seasonings, tomato purée and sugar. Pour the liquid over the chicken and add the mushrooms. Cover and cook in the oven for 1½ hours or until the chicken is tender. Arrange the chicken in a serving dish and keep warm. Thicken the cooking liquid to the desired consistency using the cornflour paste and pour over the chicken.

Cals 367   20 mins   1½ hours

Chicken & Turkey

Serves 4

CRÊPES *Florentino*

For the Pancakes:

3oz (75g) plain flour – sifted
1 egg – size 3
2 tsp (10ml) Schwartz Italian Seasoning
7fl oz (200ml) milk
A little cooking oil for frying
2oz (50g) butter or margarine
12oz (350g) boneless chicken – diced
1 large onion – chopped
10oz (275g) packet frozen chopped
   spinach – cooked and drained
6 tbs (90ml) single cream

3 tbs (45ml) Parmesan cheese
Salt and Schwartz Ground White Pepper
For the Sauce:
1oz (25g) butter or margarine
1oz (25g) plain flour
1 pint (600ml) milk
2 tbs (30ml) Parmesan cheese
Salt and Schwartz Ground White Pepper

To prepare the pancakes, place the flour in a bowl and stir in the egg and 1 tsp (5ml) Italian Seasoning. Blend in the milk to form a smooth batter. Use to make 8 small pancakes and cook in the usual way using a lightly oiled frying pan. Put to one side.

For the filling, melt the butter or margarine in a frying pan and fry the chicken and onion until cooked throughout. Using a mincer or food processor, mince the chicken and onion with the spinach. Stir in the cream, Parmesan cheese and remaining 1 tsp (5ml) Italian Seasoning. Add salt and White Pepper to taste. Divide the mixture between the 8 pancakes, roll up and place in an ovenproof dish.

Preheat oven to 400°F, 200°C, Gas Mark 6.

To make the sauce, melt the butter or margarine in a saucepan, stir in the flour and cook for 1 minute. Blend in the milk and bring to the boil, stirring. Stir in 1 tbs (15ml) Parmesan cheese and salt and White Pepper to taste. Pour over the pancakes and sprinkle with the remaining Parmesan cheese. Place in the oven for 20-25 minutes or until hot and golden.

Accompany with salad or vegetables and serve as a main course or starter.

Cals 688   40 mins   25 mins

Handy hint for garlic lovers
Just replace the Italian Seasoning in the above recipe with
Schwartz Garlic Italian Seasoning.

Chicken & Turkey

Chicken & Turkey

Serves 4

Malaysian CURRY

2 tbs (30ml) cooking oil
4 large boneless chicken breasts – skinned
 and cut in half
1 medium onion – sliced
2 tbs (30ml) Schwartz Mild Authentic
 Curry Blend
1 tbs (15ml) plain flour

½ pint (300ml) chicken stock
¼ tsp (1.25ml) salt
¼ pint (150ml) single cream or natural
 yoghurt
1oz (25g) creamed coconut – flaked
14oz (400g) tin mango slices – drained
½oz (15g) flaked almonds – toasted

Heat the oil in a frying pan and fry the chicken and onion until lightly browned. Add the Curry Blend and cook gently for 1 minute. Stir in the flour and cook for a further minute. Blend in the stock and salt and bring to the boil, stirring continuously. Cover and simmer gently for 30 minutes or until the chicken is tender. Stir in the cream or yoghurt, coconut and mango slices. Heat through gently before serving. Sprinkle with the flaked almonds.

Cals 413   10 mins   30 mins

Serves 4

Nasi GORENG

12oz (350g) long grain white rice
2 tbs (30ml) sesame or vegetable oil
1lb (450g) turkey breast fillets – diced
1 large carrot – peeled and thinly sliced
1 small red pepper – diced
2 tsp (10ml) Schwartz Chinese Five Spice
 Seasoning
½ tsp (2.5ml) Schwartz Ground
 Coriander

½ tsp (2.5ml) Schwartz Ground Ginger
½ tsp (2.5ml) Schwartz Garlic Granules
¼ tsp (1.25ml) Schwartz Cayenne
 Pepper
4 tbs (60ml) dark soy sauce
1½ tsp (7.5ml) caster sugar
6oz (175g) fresh beansprouts
1 bunch spring onions – sliced
4oz (100g) cooked shelled prawns

Cook the rice in boiling salted water until just tender. Drain. Heat the oil in a large frying pan or wok and stir-fry the turkey for 5 minutes, adding the carrot and red pepper for the last minute. Add the spices and cook for a few seconds, stirring. Add the remaining ingredients and cooked rice. Cook over a high heat for a further 4-5 minutes, stirring continuously.

Cals 587   20 mins   10 mins

Chicken & Turkey

Malaysian Curry top, Nasi Goreng below.

RUSSIA *Serves 4*

TURKEY *Kiev*

3oz (75g) butter
1 tsp (5ml) Schwartz Chives
½ tsp (2.5ml) Schwartz Garlic Granules
A few drops of lemon juice
2 large turkey breast fillets
4 slices cooked ham

3 eggs – size 3 – beaten
6oz (175g) fresh white breadcrumbs and
2 tsp (10ml) Schwartz Chicken Seasoning
   mixed together
Cooking oil – for deep frying

Blend the butter with the Chives, Garlic Granules and lemon juice. Using a sharp knife, cut each turkey fillet in half widthways and then slice through horizontally to make 8 pieces. Pound with a rolling pin to form thin 'escalopes'. Cut the ham into 8 pieces, the same size as the escalopes. Place on top of the escalopes and spread with the Garlic butter. Roll up tightly and chill in the refrigerator for 30 minutes or until the butter is very firm. Coat each turkey roll in beaten egg and toss in the seasoned breadcrumbs. Coat again with the beaten egg and breadcrumbs so that the turkey is thoroughly covered. Deep fry in hot oil for 5-6 minutes or until golden and cooked throughout. Drain on absorbent kitchen paper and serve hot with sautéd potatoes and fresh vegetables or salad.

Cals 561   25 mins + 30 mins chilling time   10 mins

FRANCE

Serves 4-6 LAYERED TURKEY *Terrine*

8 rashers streaky bacon
1lb (450g) turkey breast fillets – skinned
   and minced
8oz (225g) pork sausagemeat
4oz (100g) chicken livers – minced
4oz (100g) onion – finely chopped
2oz (50g) fresh white breadcrumbs

2 tsp (10ml) Schwartz Basil
½ tsp (2.5ml) salt
¼ tsp (1.25ml) Schwartz Ground White
   Pepper
1 egg – size 3 – beaten
3oz (75g) broccoli florets – chopped
6oz (175g) tomatoes – skinned and sliced

Preheat oven to 350°F, 180°C, Gas Mark 4.

Line the sides and bottom of a greased 2lb (900g) loaf tin with the bacon. Thoroughly mix the turkey, sausagemeat, liver, onion, breadcrumbs, seasonings and egg. Fill the tin with alternate layers of the turkey mixture, broccoli and tomatoes, starting and finishing with a layer of the turkey mixture. Wrap the tin in foil and place in a deep baking tin, half filled with boiling water. Cook in the oven for 2 hours.

Drain excess liquid from the terrine and press with a heavy weight until cool. Refrigerate for 1–2 hours or overnight.

Turn out the terrine and cut into slices for serving.

Cals 360-540    25 mins   2 hours + cooling time

Pastitsio left, Spicy Minced Beef Tacos right, see over for recipes.

Beef
& Mince

Beef & Mince

Makes 12 Spicy MINCED BEEF *Tacos*

1lb (450g) minced beef
1 medium onion – finely chopped
1 tsp (5ml) plain flour
¼ pint (150ml) beef stock
2 tsp (10ml) Schwartz Mild Chili Powder
1 tsp (5ml) Schwartz Oregano
½ tsp (2.5ml) Schwartz Garlic Granules

½ tsp (2.5ml) salt
1 tbs (15ml) tomato purée
1 small green pepper – diced
To serve:
12 taco shells
Shredded lettuce and chopped tomatoes
Sour cream, mayonnaise or grated cheese

Fry the minced beef and onion until browned. Add the flour and cook for 1 minute, stirring. Blend in the stock, seasonings and tomato purée. Add the green pepper and bring to the boil, stirring. Simmer, uncovered, for 15 to 20 minutes or until almost all the liquid has evaporated. Stir occasionally. Divide the mince mixture between the taco shells, top with lettuce and tomato and finish with a little sour cream, mayonnaise or grated cheese.

Cals 129 per taco 10 mins 20 mins

Serves 4 PASTITSIO

6oz (175g) macaroni
1lb (450g) minced beef
1 medium onion – finely chopped
14oz (400g) tin chopped tomatoes
2 tbs (30ml) tomato purée
1½ tsp (7.5ml) Schwartz Oregano
½ tsp (2.5ml) Schwartz Ground Allspice
¼ tsp (1.25ml) Schwartz Minced Garlic
¾ tsp (3.75ml) salt

For the topping:
2oz (50g) butter
2oz (50g) plain flour
½ pint (300ml) milk
¼ tsp (1.25ml) Schwartz Cayenne
   Pepper
6oz (175g) Cheddar cheese – grated
¼ pint (150ml) natural yoghurt
1 egg – size 3 – beaten

Cook the macaroni in boiling salted water until tender. Drain. Fry the minced beef and onion until browned.
Stir in the tomatoes, tomato purée and seasonings. Bring to the boil, cover and simmer for 15 minutes.
To prepare the topping, melt the butter, add the flour and cook for 1 minute. Blend in the milk and bring to the boil, stirring. Remove from the heat and stir in the Cayenne Pepper, 4oz (100g) of the cheese, yoghurt and egg.
Preheat oven to 350°F, 180°C, Gas Mark 4.
Combine the macaroni and minced beef in an ovenproof dish. Pour over the topping and sprinkle with the remaining cheese. Bake for 35-40 minutes or until golden. Stand for 5-10 minutes before serving.

✳ Cals 797 30 mins 40 mins

Beef & Mince

Yorkshire Dales STEAK & KIDNEY PIE

Serves 4

2 tbs (30ml) cooking oil
1lb (450g) lean stewing steak – cubed
10oz (275g) lambs kidneys – cored and
   quartered
6oz (175g) onions – sliced
1oz (25g) plain flour
½ pint (300ml) beef stock
1½ tsp (7.5ml) Schwartz Mixed Herbs
½ tsp (2.5ml) Schwartz Thyme

¼ tsp (1.25ml) Schwartz Onion Salt
¼ tsp (1.25ml) Schwartz Ground Black
   Pepper
2 tsp (10ml) tomato purée
8oz (225g) mushrooms – sliced
7oz (200g) packet puff pastry
Beaten egg – to glaze
Schwartz Sesame Seeds – to garnish

Heat the oil in a large saucepan and fry the meat, kidneys and onions until lightly browned. Add the flour and cook for 1 minute, stirring. Blend in the stock, seasonings and tomato purée. Add the mushrooms and bring to the boil, stirring. Cover and simmer very gently for 2 hours or until the meat is tender, stirring occasionally. Transfer to a 2 pint (1.1 litre) pie dish and allow to cool.

Preheat oven to 425°F, 220°C, Gas Mark 7.

Roll out the pastry and make a pie lid in the usual way. Brush with beaten egg and sprinkle lightly with Sesame Seeds. Cook for 20-25 minutes or until the pastry is risen and golden brown.

Cals 555 25 mins 2½ hrs

Beef & Mince

FRANCE

Serves 4 # BEEF *Bourguignon*

2 tbs (30ml) cooking oil
1½lb (675g) lean stewing steak – cubed
Approx 7fl oz (200ml) beef stock
1oz (25g) butter
4oz (100g) streaky bacon – chopped
4oz (100g) button mushrooms
6oz (175g) shallots – peeled

1½oz (40g) plain flour
½ pint (300ml) red wine
2 tsp (10ml) Schwartz Herbes de Provence
¼ tsp (1.25ml) Schwartz Minced Garlic
¼ tsp (1.25ml) salt
Pinch of Schwartz Ground Black Pepper

Preheat oven to 350°F, 180°C, Gas Mark 4.

Heat the oil in a pan, brown the meat and transfer to a casserole dish using a slotted spoon. Drain the meat juices from the pan into a measuring jug and make up to ½ pint (300ml) with beef stock.

Melt the butter and fry the bacon, mushrooms and shallots for 2-3 minutes. Add the flour and cook for 1 minute. Blend in the stock, wine and seasonings. Bring to the boil, stirring. Pour over the meat, cover and cook in the oven for 2 hours.

Cals 612   20 mins   2 hours

Handy Hint for Beef Bourguignon

For a simple Beef Bourguignon see the recipe idea on the back of the Schwartz Authentic Mix pack for Beef Casserole.

ITALY

Serves 4 # MEATBALLS *Milanese*

For the meatballs:
1lb (450g) minced beef
2oz (50g) fresh white breadcrumbs
1 egg – size 3 – beaten
1 tsp (5ml) Schwartz Italian Seasoning
½ tsp (2.5ml) salt

For the sauce:
1 medium onion – finely chopped
1 tbs (15ml) cooking oil
14oz (400g) tin chopped tomatoes

1 small red pepper – sliced
½oz (15g) plain flour
½ pint (300ml) beef stock
2 tbs (30ml) tomato purée
1 tsp (5ml) Schwartz Italian Seasoning
¼ tsp (1.25ml) Schwartz Garlic Granules
Salt and Schwartz Ground Black Pepper – to taste
1oz (25g) black olives – stoned and sliced

Preheat oven to 400°F, 200°C, Gas Mark 6.

Prepare meatballs by mixing the ingredients together. Shape into 24 small balls. Cook on a baking sheet in the oven for 20 minutes.

To prepare the sauce, soften the onion in the oil, add all the remaining ingredients and bring to the boil, stirring. Add the meatballs and simmer for 5 minutes.

Cals 397   20 mins   25 mins

Beef & Mince

Beef Bourguignon top, Meatballs Milanese below.

Pork Satay, see over for recipe.

Lamb
& Pork

Lamb & Pork

Serves 4

PORK *Satay*

For the marinade:
2 tbs (30ml) cooking oil
3 tbs (45ml) soy sauce
1 tsp (5ml) tomato purée
1 tsp (5ml) light brown sugar
½ tsp (2.5ml) Schwartz Hot Chili
Powder
1lb (450g) lean pork – cut into small cubes

For the sauce:
2 tsp (10ml) cooking oil
½ tsp (2.5ml) Schwartz Ground Ginger
¼ tsp (1.25ml) Schwartz Hot Chili
Powder
3oz (75g) crunchy peanut butter
½ pint (300ml) boiling water
1 tsp (5ml) light brown sugar
½oz (15g) creamed coconut
1 tsp (5ml) Schwartz Minced Onion
¼ tsp (1.25ml) salt
2 tsp (10ml) lemon juice

Combine the marinade ingredients in a bowl. Add the meat, stir well, cover and refrigerate for 2 hours or overnight.

Thread the meat onto small wooden or metal skewers and grill for 6-8 minutes, turning frequently until tender.

To make the sauce, heat the oil in a small saucepan, add the Ginger, Hot Chili Powder and peanut butter and cook for 1 minute. Remove from the heat and stir in the boiling water, sugar, creamed coconut, Minced Onion and salt. Bring to the boil, stirring. Simmer gently for 5-6 minutes or until the sauce is of the desired consistency. At the end of cooking, stir in the lemon juice.

Arrange the skewered pork on a plate, pour a little of the sauce over the meat and serve the remainder separately.

Cals 406 25 mins + 2 hrs marinating 10 mins

Handy Hint for Chop Suey

For a really quick and tasty stir-fry use Schwartz Authentic Mix for Chop Suey from the large range of Schwartz packet mixes.

Thin strips of lean pork and vegetables, flavoured with Schwartz special blend of Chinese spices, gives this dish an authentic flavour.

Lamb & Pork

CHINA

Serves 4   ## Chinese-style SPARE RIBS

2lb (900g) Chinese-style spare ribs
3 tbs (45ml) Worcestershire sauce
3 tbs (45ml) tomato ketchup
3 tbs (45ml) soy sauce
3 tbs (45ml) clear honey
3 tbs (45ml) apricot jam

1 tsp (5ml) Schwartz Chinese Five Spice
  Seasoning
¼ tsp (1.25ml) mustard powder
15oz (425g) tin pineapple pieces – drained

Preheat oven to 400°F, 200°C, Gas Mark 6.

Place the spare ribs in a saucepan of boiling water for 10 minutes, then drain and transfer to a foil-lined roasting tin. Place the Worcestershire sauce, ketchup, soy sauce, honey, jam, Chinese Five Spice Seasoning and mustard in a small saucepan. Heat gently until smooth, pour over the ribs and place in the oven for 40 minutes. Occasionally baste the ribs with the sauce throughout cooking. Add the pineapple pieces and increase the oven temperature to 425°F, 220°C, Gas Mark 7 and cook for a further 15-20 minutes until the sauce has thickened to form a glaze on the meat.

Serve as a starter or as part of a Chinese meal.

Cals 486   15 mins   1 hour

Lamb & Pork

Cassoulet top, Normandy Pork below.

Lamb & Pork

FRANCE

Serves 4-6

Quick CASSOULET

1 tbs (15ml) cooking oil
3oz (75g) streaky bacon – chopped
1 medium onion – finely chopped
4oz (100g) French garlic sausage –
    roughly chopped
4 large Frankfurter sausages – sliced
2 x 14oz (400g) tins baked beans
2 tsp (10ml) Schwartz Herbes de
    Provence

¾ tsp (3.75ml) Schwartz Onion Pepper
1 tbs (15ml) tomato purée
¼ pint (150ml) chicken stock
1 tsp (5ml) Schwartz Garlic Bread
    Seasoning and 2oz (50g) butter blended
    together
Approximately 6 slices French bread

    Heat the oil in a saucepan and fry the bacon and onion for 3-4 minutes. Stir in the garlic sausage, Frankfurter sausages, baked beans, Herbes de Provence, Onion Pepper, tomato purée and chicken stock. Bring to the boil, cover and simmer for 20 minutes, stirring occasionally. Transfer to an ovenproof dish. Spread the garlic butter over the French bread and place on top of the casserole. Place under a hot grill for 1-2 minutes or until the bread is lightly browned.

Cals 546-820   15 mins   25 mins

FRANCE

Serves 4

Normandy PORK

3 tbs (45ml) cooking oil
4 pork chops – trimmed of excess fat
1 medium onion – thinly sliced
1½oz (40g) plain flour
½ pint (300ml) chicken stock
7fl oz (200ml) carton pure apple juice
1 tsp (5ml) Schwartz Rubbed Sage

½ tsp (2.5ml) salt
¼ tsp (1.25ml) Schwartz Citrus Pepper
¼ tsp (1.25ml) Schwartz Ground Ginger
2 eating apples – cored and sliced
2 tbs (30ml) Calvados – optional

    Preheat oven to 350°F, 180°C, Gas Mark 4.
    Heat the oil in a frying pan, brown the chops and transfer to a casserole dish using a slotted spoon. Add the onion to the oil remaining in the pan and fry until softened. Add the flour and cook for 1 minute, stirring. Gradually blend in the stock and apple juice and bring to the boil, stirring. Add the seasonings and pour over the chops. Cover the casserole and cook in the oven for 1½ hours or until the meat is tender, adding the apple slices and Calvados, if using, for the last 20 minutes of cooking.

Cals 613   15 mins   1½ hours

Lamb & Pork

INDIA

Serves 4

Rogan JOSH

2 tbs (30ml) cooking oil
1½lb (675g) lean lamb – cubed
1 large onion – sliced
2 tbs (30ml) Schwartz Medium Authentic
   Curry Blend

¼ pint (150ml) natural yoghurt and
1 tsp (5ml) plain flour – blended together
14oz (400g) tin chopped tomatoes
1 tbs (15ml) tomato purée
2 tsp (10ml) Schwartz Garam Masala

Preheat oven to 350°F, 180°C, Gas Mark 4.

Heat the oil in a frying pan and fry the meat and onion until browned. Add the Curry Blend and cook for 1 minute, stirring. Stir in the yoghurt and flour, tomatoes and tomato purée. Bring to the boil and transfer to a casserole dish. Cover and cook in the oven for 1½ hours or until the meat is tender. At the end of cooking, stir in the Garam Masala.

Cals 384 15 mins 1½ hours

Handy Hint for Madras Curry

Use Schwartz Authentic Mix for Madras Curry, from the large range of Schwartz packet mixes, to make a delicious curry with a little more heat.

MIDDLE EAST

Spiced LAMB & AUBERGINE Koftas

Serves 4

For the Tomato Dip :
3 tbs (45ml) tomato purée
4 tbs (60ml) cold water
1 tsp (5ml) brown sugar
1 tsp (5ml) vinegar
¼ tsp (1.25ml) Schwartz Hot Chili
   Powder
¼ tsp (1.25ml) Schwartz Mint

For the Koftas :
3 tbs (45ml) cooking oil
8oz (225g) aubergine – finely diced
12oz (350g) minced lamb
2oz (50g) fresh white breadcrumbs
2 tsp (10ml) tomato purée
2 tsp (10ml) Schwartz Ground Cumin
1 tsp (5ml) Schwartz Ground Allspice
1 tsp (5ml) Schwartz Hot Chili Powder
¾ tsp (3.75ml) salt

To prepare the dip, place all ingredients in a small saucepan and simmer gently for 1 minute. Cool.

To prepare the koftas fry the aubergine in oil until soft. Drain and cool. Combine the lamb with the breadcrumbs, tomato purée, Cumin, Allspice, Chili Powder and salt. Stir in the aubergine and mix thoroughly. Divide the mixture into 8 pieces and roll into 'sausage' shapes. Push a wooden or metal skewer through the length of the 'sausage' to form a kofta. Cook for 10-15 minutes under a preheated grill, turning occasionally until cooked throughout. Accompany with the tomato dip and a crisp salad.

Cals 381 25 mins 15 mins

Lamb & Pork

Rogan Josh top, Spiced Lamb & Aubergine Koftas below.

Lamb & Pork

ROAST LAMB with *Garlic & Rosemary*

Serves 6–8

*1 leg of lamb – approximately 3½lb
   (1.5kg) in weight
1oz (25g) butter – melted
½ tsp (2.5ml) Schwartz Garlic Granules*

*1 tsp (5ml) Schwartz Rosemary
1 packet Schwartz Orange and Rosemary
   Gravy Mix*

Preheat oven to 350°F, 180°C, Gas Mark 4.

Brush the lamb with the melted butter and sprinkle evenly with the Garlic Granules and Rosemary. Place on a rack in a roasting tin and cover lightly with aluminium foil. Cook for 30 minutes per 1lb (450g) plus an additional 30 minutes. Remove the foil half way through cooking to allow the fat to become crisp and golden. At the end of cooking, remove the joint from the oven and allow to stand for 5 minutes before carving. Prepare the Orange and Rosemary Gravy Mix as directed on the packet and use to accompany the sliced meat.

Cals 506-674   10 mins   2½ hours

Lamb & Pork

Serves 4

Navarin of LAMB

3 tbs (45ml) cooking oil
12 lamb cutlets – trimmed of excess fat
6oz (175g) button onions – peeled
1½oz (40g) plain flour
¾ pint (450ml) chicken stock
1 tsp (5ml) Schwartz Mint
¾ tsp (3.75ml) salt

¼ tsp (1.25ml) Schwartz Ground White
   Pepper
1 tbs (15ml) tomato purée
6oz (175g) baby carrots – scraped
8oz (225g) small new potatoes
4oz (100g) frozen peas

Preheat oven to 350°F, 180°C, Gas Mark 4.
Heat the oil in a frying pan, brown the cutlets and onions and transfer to a casserole dish using a slotted spoon. Add the flour to the frying pan and cook for 1 minute, stirring. Gradually blend in the stock and bring to the boil, stirring. Stir the Mint, salt, White Pepper and tomato purée into the sauce and pour over the meat and onions. Add the carrots and potatoes, cover the and cook in the oven for 1½ hours or until the meat is tender. Add the peas for the last 30 minutes of cooking.

Cals 652   20 mins   1½ hours

Fish
& Seafood

Fish & Seafood

SPAIN

Serves 4

PAELLA

1 tbs (15ml) cooking oil
1oz (25g) butter or margarine
12oz (350g) boneless chicken – pieces
1 medium onion – sliced
12oz (350g) long grain white rice
Half a sachet Schwartz Saffron strands –
   lightly crushed between fingertips
Large pinch of Schwartz Cayenne Pepper
1 tsp (5ml) Schwartz Garlic Granules
¼ tsp (1.25ml) salt

1¼ pints (750ml) chicken stock
1 red pepper – sliced
1 green pepper – sliced
4oz (100g) frozen peas – cooked
4oz (100g) cooked shelled prawns
1oz (25g) whole black olives
12 mussels – thoroughly cleaned and
   beards removed
A few whole prawns and lemon wedges to
   garnish

Heat the oil and butter or margarine in a large frying pan or paella pan, add the chicken and onion and fry until lightly browned. Add the rice and cook for a further 1-2 minutes, stirring. Stir in the Saffron strands, Cayenne Pepper, Garlic Granules, salt, chicken stock and the red and green peppers. Bring to the boil and simmer, uncovered, for 25-30 minutes or until the rice is tender and all the liquid is absorbed. Stir occasionally and add a little extra water if necessary. 5 minutes before the end of cooking, stir in the peas, prawns and olives.

Meanwhile, place the mussels in a saucepan of boiling water. Boil until all the shells are open (approximately 5 minutes). Discard any unopened mussels. Use to garnish the cooked paella, together with the whole prawns and lemon wedges.

The fresh mussels may be replaced with a small tin of mussels in brine. Simply rinse the mussels and stir into the paella just before serving.

Cals 588   30 mins   30 mins

Handy Hint for Fishermans Pie

A deliciously creamy dish with a hint of nutmeg and herbs can be made using Schwartz Authentic Mix for Fishermans Pie.

Handy Hint for Grilled or Poached Fish

Schwartz Dill Pepper, in its distinctive black capped jar, tastes particularly good sprinkled on poached or grilled fish, especially salmon.

Fish & Seafood

FRANCE

Serves 4-6 Smoked HADDOCK Quiche

6oz (175g) short crust pastry
6oz (175g) smoked haddock – cooked and flaked
1 small courgette – thinly sliced
3oz (75g) Cheddar cheese – grated

3 eggs – size 3
7fl oz (200ml) milk
1 tsp (5ml) Schwartz Dill Pepper
¼ tsp (1.25ml) Schwartz Ground Nutmeg

Preheat oven to 400°F, 200°C, Gas Mark 6.

Roll out the pastry and use to line a 9" (225mm) flan dish. Bake blind for 15-20 minutes.

Place the fish and courgettes in the bottom of the flan case and sprinkle over the cheese. Beat the eggs thoroughly, blend in the milk, Dill Pepper and Nutmeg. Pour over the fish and return to the oven for 30-35 minutes or until lightly golden and firm to the touch. Serve hot or cold.

Cals 266-400   20 mins   35 mins

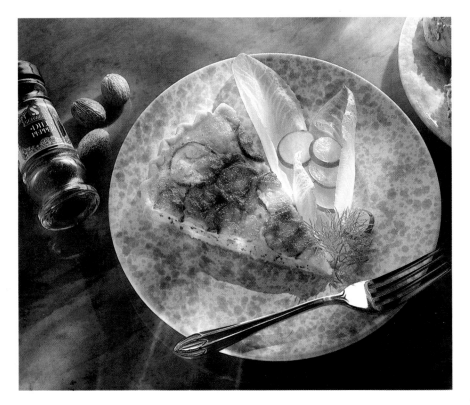

FRANCE

Serves 4

PLAICE Veronique

4 large or 8 small plaice fillets – skinned
Approximately ¾ pint (450ml) milk
1oz (25g) butter or margarine
1 small onion – thinly sliced
1oz (25g) plain flour
1 tsp (5ml) Schwartz Tarragon

½ tsp (2.5ml) Schwartz Thyme
5 tsp (25ml) lemon juice
4oz (100g) green grapes – cut in half and
    deseeded
Salt and Schwartz Ground White Pepper

Roll up the plaice fillets and place in a frying pan. Pour over ½ pint (300ml) milk and bring to the boil. Cover and simmer gently for 8-10 minutes or until the fish is tender. Transfer the fish to a serving dish and keep warm. Pour the cooking liquid into a measuring jug and make up to ¾ pint (450ml) with the remaining milk. Melt the butter or margarine in the frying pan and gently fry the onion until softened. Add the flour and cook for 1 minute, stirring. Blend in the milk and bring to the boil, stirring. Stir in the Tarragon, Thyme and lemon juice. Cover and simmer gently for 5 minutes. Stir half the grapes into the sauce and season to taste with the salt and White Pepper. Pour the sauce over the fish and garnish with the remaining grapes.

Cals 315   15 mins   15 mins

Fish & Seafood

Serves 4

FISH Creole

1 tbs (15ml) cooking oil
1 medium onion – finely chopped
2 tsp (10ml) Schwartz Garam Masala
1 tsp (5ml) Schwartz Ground Ginger
½ tsp (2.5ml) Schwartz Ground Allspice
14oz (400g) tin chopped tomatoes
2 tbs (30ml) tomato purée

1 tsp (5ml) granulated sugar
½ tsp (2.5ml) salt
¼ tsp (1.25ml) Schwartz Minced Garlic
Pinch of Schwartz Cayenne Pepper
¼ pint (150ml) water
8oz (225g) tin pineapple pieces – drained
1lb (450g) cod fillet – skinned and cubed

Heat the oil in a frying pan and fry the onion until softened. Add the Garam Masala, Ginger and Allspice and cook for 1 minute, stirring. Add the tomatoes, tomato purée, sugar, salt, Minced Garlic, Cayenne Pepper and water. Bring to the boil, stirring. Simmer gently, uncovered, for 10 minutes. Stir in the pineapple and cod. Cover and simmer for a further 10 minutes or until the fish is tender.

If a hotter flavour is desired, add an extra pinch of Cayenne Pepper.

Cals 193 10 mins 20 mins

Winter Vegetable Goulash left, Cauliflower and Tomato Madras right, see over for recipes.

Versatile
Vegetables

Versatile Vegetables

CAULIFLOWER & TOMATO Madras

Serves 4

1 medium cauliflower – divided into florets
4oz (100g) green beans
1 tbs (15ml) cooking oil
1 large onion – sliced
2 tbs (30ml) Schwartz Medium or Hot
   Authentic Curry Blend
2 tbs (30ml) tomato purée

¼ pint (150ml) vegetable stock
½ tsp (2.5ml) salt
¼ pint (150ml) single cream or yoghurt
14oz (400g) tin chick peas – drained
12oz (350g) tomatoes – skinned, deseeded
   and chopped

Cook the cauliflower and green beans in boiling salted water for 8-10 minutes or until tender. Drain and reserve.

Heat the oil in a frying pan and fry the onion until softened. Add the Curry Blend and cook gently for 30 seconds, stirring. Stir in the tomato purée, stock, salt and the cream or yoghurt. Add the vegetables, bring to the boil and simmer, uncovered, for 5 minutes, stirring occasionally.

Cals 353   15 mins   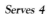10 mins

WINTER VEGETABLE Goulash

Serves 4

1 tbs (15ml) cooking oil
2 medium onions – sliced
8oz (225g) carrots – peeled and sliced
8oz (225g) potatoes – peeled and diced
8oz (225g) parsnips – peeled and sliced
1 red pepper – sliced
4 sticks of celery – sliced
1oz (25g) butter or margarine

1½oz (40g) plain flour
¾ pint (450ml) vegetable stock
14oz (400g) tin tomatoes
3 tbs (45ml) tomato purée
5 tsp (25ml) Schwartz Hot Paprika
½ tsp (2.5ml) Schwartz Marjoram
¼ tsp (1.25ml) salt
2 tbs (30ml) sour cream

Preheat oven to 180°C, 350°F, Gas Mark 4.

Heat the oil in a frying pan and soften the onions and carrots. Transfer to a casserole dish using a slotted spoon. Add the remaining vegetables to the casserole. Melt the butter or margarine in the frying pan. Add the flour and cook for 1 minute. Gradually blend in the stock, tomatoes, tomato purée and seasonings. Bring to the boil, stirring. Pour over the vegetables, cover and cook in the oven for 1½-2 hours or until the vegetables are tender. Just before serving, stir in the sour cream.

Cals 266   20 mins   2 hours

SPINACH & RICOTTA *Lasagne*

Serves 4

ITALY

3oz (75g) butter or margarine
4oz (100g) onion – finely chopped
4oz (100g) mushrooms – finely chopped
1lb (450g) frozen spinach – cooked,
   drained and finely chopped
8oz (225g) Ricotta cheese
1 tsp (5ml) Schwartz Basil
½ tsp (2.5ml) Schwartz Garlic Granules

¼ tsp (1.25ml) Schwartz Ground
   Nutmeg
Salt and Schwartz Ground Black Pepper
2oz (50g) plain flour
1 pint (600ml) milk
4-6 sheets lasagne pasta – cooked and
   drained
1oz (25g) Parmesan cheese

Melt 1oz (25g) butter or margarine in a saucepan and gently fry
the onion and mushrooms for 3-4 minutes. Stir in the spinach, Ricotta
cheese, Basil, Garlic Granules and Nutmeg. Season to taste with salt and
Black Pepper and put aside. Melt the remaining butter or margarine in a
saucepan, add the flour and cook for 1 minute. Remove from the heat
and blend in the milk. Bring to the boil, stirring. Season to taste with
salt and Black Pepper.

   Preheat oven to 400°F, 200°C, Gas Mark 6. Spread half the
spinach mixture in the bottom of a lightly greased ovenproof dish. Top
with a layer of lasagne, followed by half the white sauce. Repeat. Sprinkle
with Parmesan cheese and place in oven for 30 minutes or until golden.

Cals 509   30 mins   30 mins

Serves 6–8   ## *Spiced* RED CABBAGE

2oz (50g) butter or margarine
2 medium onions – finely chopped
1 medium red cabbage – approximately 2lb
  (900g) in weight
2 tbs (30ml) red wine vinegar
1 tsp (5ml) salt
½ tsp (2.5ml) Schwartz Ground Nutmeg

½ tsp (2.5ml) Schwartz Mixed Spice
¼ tsp (1.25ml) Schwartz Ground Black
  Pepper
2 medium cooking apples – peeled and
  sliced
2oz (50g) sultanas

Preheat oven to 350°F, 180°C, Gas Mark 4.

Heat the butter or margarine in a large saucepan and gently fry the onions for 2-3 minutes. Finely chop the red cabbage and add to the saucepan. Stir in the vinegar, salt, Nutmeg, Mixed Spice and Black Pepper. Continue to cook for 3-4 minutes, stirring frequently. Add the apple and transfer to an ovenproof dish. Cover and cook in the oven for 1 hour or until the red cabbage is tender. Stir in the sultanas at the end of cooking.

Serve hot with chicken, turkey, beef or pork dishes or warm with cold sliced meats.

Cals 100-134   10 mins   1 hour

Versatile Vegetables

Serves 4

RATATOUILLE

2 tbs (30ml) olive oil
1 medium onion – thinly sliced
8oz (225g) courgettes – thinly sliced
1 medium aubergine – thinly sliced
1 red pepper – sliced
8oz (225g) tin chopped tomatoes

2 tbs (30ml) tomato purée
½ tsp (2.5ml) Schwartz Garlic Granules
½ tsp (2.5ml) Schwartz Basil
¼ tsp (1.25ml) granulated sugar
Salt and Schwartz Ground Black Pepper

Heat the oil in a saucepan and fry the onion until softened. Stir in the remaining vegetables, tomato purée, Garlic Granules, Basil and sugar. Cover and simmer for 20-25 minutes or until the vegetables are tender. Season to taste with salt and Black Pepper before serving.

Serve as a vegetable accompaniment or sprinkle with grated cheese and serve with crusty bread or baked potatoes.

Cals 109   10 mins   25 mins

Hints and Tips

Baked POTATO TOPPINGS
Add a shake of your favourite Schwartz Seasoned Pepper to your usual baked potato topping. Try Herb or Onion Pepper with grated cheese, Dill Pepper with tuna fish and mayonnaise or Citrus Pepper with cooked, chopped chicken and natural yoghurt.

Stuffed MUSHROOMS
Top 8 large flat mushrooms with a knob of butter, a sprinkling of Schwartz Garlic Italian Seasoning and a few toasted white breadcrumbs. Finish with a little grated cheese and cook in a moderate oven for 10-15 minutes.

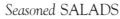

Seasoned SALADS
Liven up everyday salads by adding a good shake of Schwartz Salad Seasoning to French dressings and mayonnaise. Also, try adding to potato salads and coleslaws for an extra special flavour.

Schwartz Saffron Cake left, Baklavas right, see over for recipes.

Delicious
Desserts

Delicious Desserts

SCHWARTZ *Saffron* CAKE

Serves 6–8

For the cake:

Half a sachet of Schwartz Saffron strands
6oz (175g) butter or margarine
6oz (175g) caster sugar
3 eggs – size 3
10oz (275g) self-raising flour – sifted
4oz (100g) currants

For the filling:

8oz (225g) soft cream cheese ⎫ *blended*
1 tbs (15ml) milk ⎬ *together*
2 tbs (30ml) icing sugar ⎭
Thin strips of lemon rind – to decorate
Icing sugar – to dust

Lightly crush the Saffron strands and cover with 6 tbs (90ml) boiling water. Allow to stand for 2 hours or overnight.

Preheat oven to 325°F, 170°C, Gas Mark 3.

Grease and line a deep 7″ (175mm) cake tin. Cream the butter and sugar together. Beat in the eggs, adding a little flour if necessary. Strain the Saffron liquid and discard the strands. Gently fold half the flour into the cake mixture, followed by the Saffron liquid. Fold in the remaining flour and stir in the currants. Transfer to the prepared tin and cook for 1½–1¾ hours or until well risen and firm to the touch. Allow to cool slightly before turning out. When cold, split the cake in half and fill with ⅔ of the cream cheese mixture. Use the remainder to decorate the top of the cake together with the strips of lemon rind. Dust with icing sugar before serving.

Cals 555-739 20 mins + 2 hours infusion time 🍲 1½ hours

BAKLAVAS

Serves 6–8

3oz (75g) unsalted butter – melted
12 sheets filo pastry
6oz (175g) soft dark brown sugar
8oz (225g) chopped mixed nuts

1 tsp (5ml) Schwartz Ground Cinnamon
2 tbs (30ml) clear honey
1 Schwartz Cinnamon Stick
6 Schwartz Whole Cloves

Preheat oven to 375°F, 190°C, Gas Mark 5.

Line a greased 8″ x 11″ (200mm x 275mm) Swiss roll tin with 4 layers of lightly buttered filo pastry.

Combine 5oz (125g) brown sugar with the nuts and Cinnamon. Sprinkle half the mixture over the pastry and cover with a further 4 sheets of buttered filo pastry. Sprinkle over the remaining sugar and nut mixture. Cover with the remaining 4 sheets of buttered filo pastry. Trim the edges, score into rectangles and bake for 30 minutes or until golden.

Place the remaining sugar in a saucepan with the honey, Cinnamon Stick and Cloves. Add ¼ pint (150ml) water, bring to the boil and simmer for 10 minutes. Remove the spices and pour over the warm Baklavas. Allow to cool before cutting into pieces. Serve warm or cold, with cream if desired.

Cals 536-715 20 mins 30 mins

Delicious Desserts

INDIA   *Serves 6–8*   # ICED *Indian* DESSERT

2oz (50g) butter
2oz (50g) fresh white breadcrumbs
2oz (50g) caster sugar
½ tsp (2.5ml) Schwartz Ground Mace
6 Schwartz Whole Cardamoms – seeds
  removed and crushed
½ pint (300ml) double cream
14oz (400g) tin mangoes or apricots in
  syrup – drained

1oz (25g) blanched split almonds or
  pistachio nuts – roughly chopped
1oz (25g) dried banana flakes – roughly
  crushed
A few split almonds or pistachio nuts and
1 green apple – cored and sliced – to
  decorate

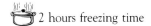

Heat the butter in a frying pan and fry the breadcrumbs until golden. Add the sugar, Mace, and crushed Cardamoms. Cook for a further minute, stirring. Allow to cool.

Whip the cream until it just holds its shape. Reserve a piece of mango or apricot for decoration and roughly chop the remainder. Stir into the cream, together with the nuts, banana flakes and breadcrumb mixture. Divide between 6 or 8 individual dessert moulds, cover and freeze for 2 hours or until firm.

Dip the moulds in hot water for a few seconds to loosen them. Turn out and decorate as desired with nuts and sliced fruit.

Cals 312-416   25 mins   2 hours freezing time

Delicious Desserts

Serves 6 # BREAD & BUTTER *Pudding*

2oz (50g) butter
8 slices of white bread – crusts removed
4oz (100g) sultanas
¾ pint (450ml) milk OR ½ pint (300ml)
  milk and ¼ pint (150ml) single cream

1½oz (40g) soft brown sugar
Grated rind of 1 orange
2 tsp (10ml) Schwartz Mixed Spice
3 eggs – size 3 – beaten
2 tbs (30ml) orange marmalade – warmed

Preheat oven to 400°F, 200°C, Gas Mark 6.
Grease a 2 pint (1.2 litres) ovenproof dish. Butter the bread and cut into triangles. Arrange layers of the bread in the dish, sprinkling the sultanas over each layer. Whisk the milk, cream (if using), sugar, orange rind and Mixed Spice into the eggs. Pour over the bread and bake for 45-50 minutes or until set. 5 minutes before the end of cooking brush the top of the pudding with the marmalade glaze. Serve hot.

Cals 369   15 mins   50 mins

Hints and Tips

Peppered STRAWBERRIES WITH ORANGE
Gently combine sliced fresh strawberries with the grated rind and juice of 2 large oranges, a sprinkling of Schwartz Citrus Pepper and a little caster sugar to taste.

Spiced YOGHURT
For a refreshing low-calorie dessert try stirring a good shake of Schwartz Ground Cinnamon, Nutmeg or Ginger into natural yoghurt.

CARDAMOM *Syrup*
Lightly crush the seeds from 10 Whole Cardamoms and add to ½ pint (300ml) water together with 2oz (50g) caster sugar. Bring to boil and simmer for 5 minutes. Allow to cool before straining to remove the spices. Delicious with all fruit salads and ice creams.

Delicious Desserts

HERB & SPICE INDEX